Grandchild, From My Heart To Yours

A Guided Journal & Family Keepsake

GrandparentsAcademy.com

Grandparent, Please Read This First

Dear grandparent,

This guided journal and keepsake was thoughtfully created to assist you with helping your family thrive for generations to come. The prompts included are designed using the Share Your V.O.I.C.E.™ framework I developed after spending over a decade serving grandparents and their families. **V.O.I.C.E. stands for: Values, Origins, Items, Counsel, and Experiences.** This framework will help you communicate what truly matters.

In addition to using this framework, I'm also inviting you to join a masterclass that provides more information and resources for sharing your stories with your loved ones beyond this book. There's no cost for you to attend, and it's available online to take at your own pace. See more details below.

Personally, I've been blessed to have several grandparents in my own life who were intentional about sharing their advice, stories, and lessons learned with me. Their contributions continue to help me thrive to this day, even though some have now passed on. What you're doing matters!

Thank you for being an intentional grandparent.

With gratitude,
~Aaron
Founder, GrandparentsAcademy.com.

Join The "Share Your Story" Masterclass ($47 Value)

Get free access to additional guidance and resources for helping you share your story with loved ones.

Scan the QR code below with your phone or tablet:

Or visit:
https://training.grandparentsacademy.com/story

Written with love for:

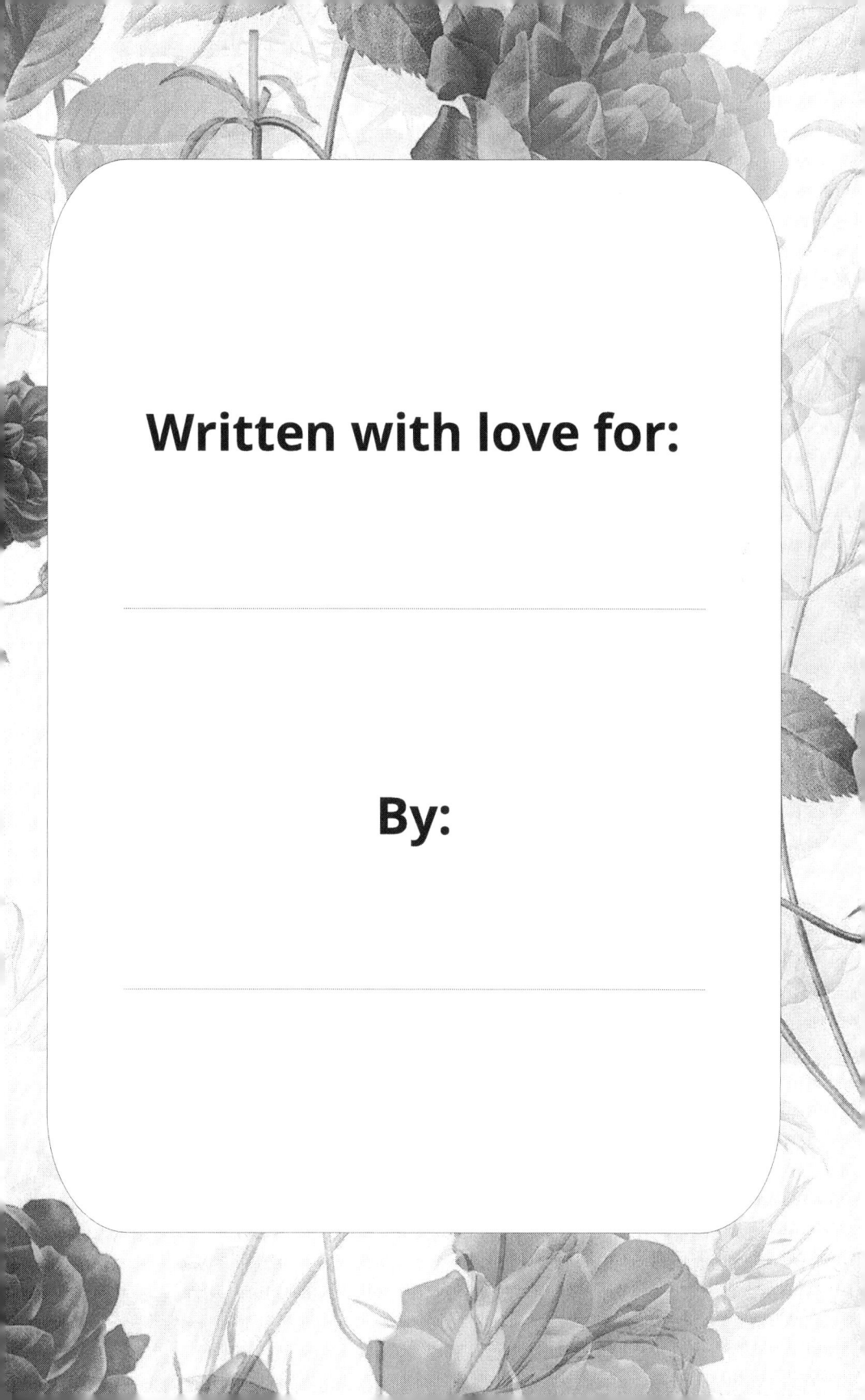

_____

By:

_____

Table of Contents

Values 7

Origins 29

Items 53

Counsel 67

Experiences 87

More Thoughts 111

Share Your V.O.I.C.E.™

Values

Grandchild, From My Heart to Yours

Values

What values do you hold most dear in your life?

_____
_____
_____
_____
_____
_____
_____
_____
_____
_____
_____
_____
_____
_____
_____
_____

"Be yourself; everyone else is already taken."
— Oscar Wilde

Grandchild, From My Heart to Yours

Values

How would you describe your faith?

"Everything comes to you at the right time. Trust the process."
— Unknown

Grandchild, From My Heart to Yours

Values

Are there any cultural or religious teachings that resonate with you deeply?

"Your purpose is not something you create; it's something you discover."
— Unknown

Grandchild, From My Heart to Yours

Values

Who or what has had the biggest influence on your core beliefs?

_____

_____

_____

_____

_____

_____

_____

_____

_____

_____

_____

_____

_____

_____

"We stand on the shoulders of those who came before us."
— Maya Angelou

Grandchild, From My Heart to Yours

Values

How have your beliefs changed over time?

"The moment we stop learning is the moment we stop growing."
— Unknown

Grandchild, From My Heart to Yours

Values

What values do you think are most important to pass on to future generations?

_____

_____

_____

_____

_____

_____

_____

_____

_____

_____

_____

_____

_____

"Legacy is not about what you own, but rather what you've grown in others."
— Aaron Larsen

Grandchild, From My Heart to Yours

Values

How have your values influenced the way you handle adversity?

"The greatest glory in living lies not in never falling, but in rising every time we fall."
— Nelson Mandela

Grandchild, From My Heart to Yours

Values

How do you define a life well lived?

"Do what makes your soul shine."
— Unknown

Grandchild, From My Heart to Yours

Values

How do you decide what is worth prioritizing in your life?

"What you focus on grows. What you neglect withers."
— Unknown

Grandchild, From My Heart to Yours

Values

What important values did you learn from your parents?

_____

_____

_____

_____

_____

_____

_____

_____

_____

_____

_____

_____

_____

_____

"Success is not what you leave to your children, but what you cultivate within them."
— Unknown

Grandchild, From My Heart to Yours

Values

What important values did you learn from your grandparents?

_____
_____
_____
_____
_____
_____
_____
_____
_____
_____
_____
_____
_____
_____
_____

"A grandparent's wisdom is a treasure that never loses its value."
— Unknown

Grandchild, From My Heart to Yours

Values

How do you define patience?

Share about a time in your life when being patient helped you.

"Trees that are slow to grow bear the best fruit."
— Molière

Grandchild, From My Heart to Yours

Values

How do you define hope?

How do you find hope when you need it most?

"You may not see it yet, but something wonderful is about to happen."
— Unknown

Grandchild, From My Heart to Yours

Values

What is courage?

How do you find courage when you're uncertain or afraid?

"Keep going. Your hardest times often lead to the greatest moments of your life."
— Unknown

Grandchild, From My Heart to Yours

Values

Share about a time when you witnessed true courage.

"Courage is resistance to fear, mastery of fear—not absence of fear."
— Mark Twain

Grandchild, From My Heart to Yours

Values

How do you define gratitude?

What are some of your favorite ways to practice gratitude?

"Gratitude is not only the greatest of virtues but the parent of all the others."
— Cicero

Grandchild, From My Heart to Yours

Values

Share about a time when you felt deep gratitude.

"Every day is a gift. That's why it's called the present."
— Unknown

Grandchild, From My Heart to Yours

Values

How do you define kindness?

What are some of your favorite ways to practice kindness?

"No act of kindness, no matter how small, is ever wasted."
— Aesop

Grandchild, From My Heart to Yours

Values

What is one of the kindest acts you've witnessed in your life?

"The world is full of kind people. If you can't find one, be one."
— *Unknown*

Grandchild, From My Heart to Yours

Values

How do you define forgiveness?

Share a meaningful moment when you were forgiven, or chose to forgive.

"The weak can never forgive. Forgiveness is the attribute of the strong."
— Mahatma Gandhi

Grandchild, From My Heart to Yours

Values

Anything else you think your grandchild should know about values?

"Live your beliefs and you can turn the world around."
— *Henry David Thoreau*

Share Your V.O.I.C.E.™

Origins

Grandchild, From My Heart to Yours

Origins

Where was your family originally from?

What do you know about the earliest members of our family?

"Family gives you the roots to stand tall and strong."
— Unknown

Grandchild, From My Heart to Yours

Origins

Do you know the meaning or history of our last names?

_____

_____

_____

_____

_____

_____

_____

_____

_____

_____

_____

_____

_____

"Blood makes you related, but love makes you family."
— Unknown

Grandchild, From My Heart to Yours

Origins

Did your family have a strong connection to a particular place?

Were there significant migrations or moves in our family history?

"Where there is family, there is love."
— Unknown

Grandchild, From My Heart to Yours

Origins

Are there any mysteries or untold stories about our family?

What do you wish you knew more about regarding our ancestors?

"Family is like music, some high notes, some low notes, but always a beautiful song."
— Unknown

Grandchild, From My Heart to Yours

Origins

Are there any family stories or legends passed down through generations?

_____
_____
_____
_____
_____
_____
_____
_____
_____
_____
_____
_____
_____
_____
_____
_____

"A family's stories are the threads that weave its history together."
— Unknown

Grandchild, From My Heart to Yours

Origins

Can you tell me about your grandparents?

_____

_____

_____

_____

_____

_____

_____

_____

_____

_____

_____

_____

_____

_____

"Grandparents, like heroes, are as necessary to a child's growth as vitamins."
— Joyce Allston

Origins

Can you describe a favorite memory with your grandparents?

"A grandparent's love is strong, endless, and unconditional."
— Unknown

Grandchild, From My Heart to Yours

Origins

What kind of work did your parents and grandparents do?

"A family's love and support is the greatest gift of all."
— *Unknown*

Grandchild, From My Heart to Yours

Origins

Were there any family members who inspired you?

"Cherish the family who inspire you, their love and wisdom are life's greatest gifts."
— *Unknown*

Grandchild, From My Heart to Yours

Origins

What historical events impacted your side of the family the most?

_____

_____

_____

_____

_____

_____

_____

_____

_____

_____

_____

_____

_____

_____

_____

"A family stitched together with love seldom unravels."
— *Unknown*

Grandchild, From My Heart to Yours

Origins

Did our family face any hardships or challenges that shaped its history?

_____
_____
_____
_____
_____
_____
_____
_____
_____
_____
_____
_____
_____
_____
_____
_____

"A family that stands together can weather any storm."
— Unknown

Grandchild, From My Heart to Yours

Origins

Were there any defining family values passed down?

"Family values are the invisible threads that bind generations together."
— Unknown

Grandchild, From My Heart to Yours

Origins

What legacy do you hope our family will continue to grow?

_____
_____
_____
_____
_____
_____
_____
_____
_____
_____
_____
_____
_____
_____
_____
_____

"What we instill in our children today becomes the legacy they carry tomorrow."
— Unknown

Grandchild, From My Heart to Yours

Origins

Describe your childhood. What was it like?

"We carry our childhood with us, not as a burden but as a treasure."
— Unknown

Grandchild, From My Heart to Yours

Origins

What traditions were important in your family growing up?

_____

_____

_____

_____

_____

_____

_____

_____

_____

_____

_____

_____

_____

_____

_____

"Family traditions are the foundation that keeps generations connected."
— Unknown

Grandchild, From My Heart to Yours

Origins

How did your family celebrate holidays or special occasions?

"The greatest gift of the holidays is time spent with those we love."
— Unknown

Grandchild, From My Heart to Yours

Origins

Did your family have any religious or spiritual traditions?

_____
_____
_____
_____
_____
_____

Were there any unique customs in your family?

_____
_____
_____
_____
_____
_____

"Traditions are the heartbeats of a family, passed down with love."
— *Unknown*

Grandchild, From My Heart to Yours

Origins

Are there any famous or notable relatives in our family tree?

_____

_____

_____

Were there any significant family achievements or honors?

_____

_____

_____

_____

_____

_____

_____

_____

_____

_____

"Family is the wind beneath your wings, lifting you higher with every achievement."
— Unknown

Grandchild, From My Heart to Yours

Origins

Describe your favorite birthday celebration.

_____
_____
_____
_____
_____
_____
_____

Were there any cherished family pets in your household?

_____
_____
_____
_____
_____
_____
_____

"A family that celebrates together, stays together."
— Unknown

Grandchild, From My Heart to Yours

Origins

Describe your best friends growing up.

"True friends are never apart, maybe in distance but never in heart."
— Unknown

Grandchild, From My Heart to Yours

Origins

How did your family handle times of war or economic struggle?

"Tough times don't last, but tough families do."
— *Unknown*

Grandchild, From My Heart to Yours

Origins

Did our family have any mottos or sayings?

_____

_____

_____

_____

_____

_____

_____

_____

_____

_____

_____

_____

_____

_____

_____

"In this family, we trust in love, faith, and each other."
— Unknown

Grandchild, From My Heart to Yours

Origins

Do we have a family crest, emblem, or seal? Can you add it below?

"A family crest is a reminder that we stand on the shoulders of giants."
— *Unknown*

Share Your V.O.I.C.E.™

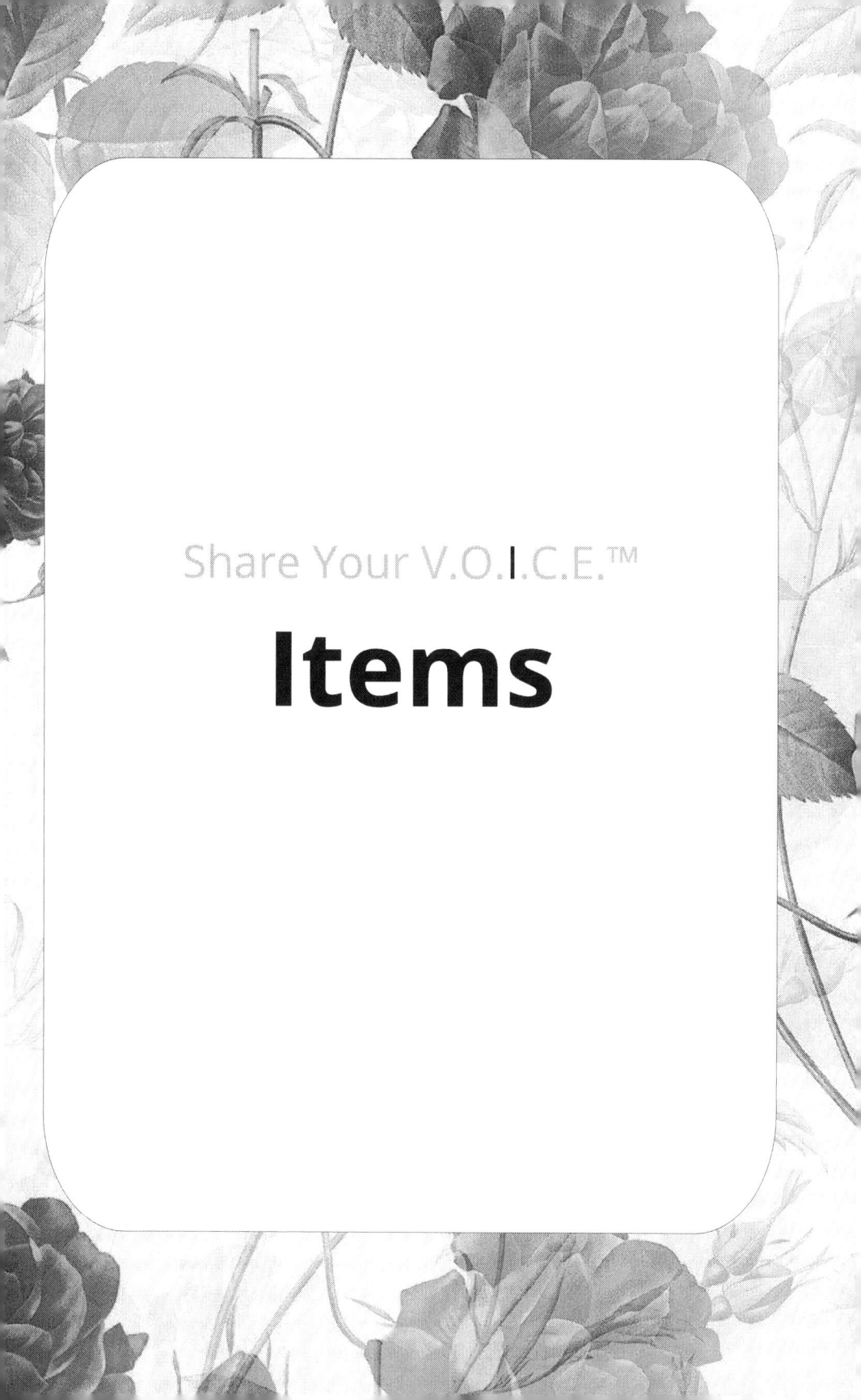

Items

Grandchild, From My Heart to Yours

Items

What is the oldest family heirloom you know of, and what's its story?

"Heirlooms are the whispers of the past, guiding the future."
— Unknown

Grandchild, From My Heart to Yours

Items

Do you have a favorite heirloom that has personal meaning to you?

_____
_____
_____
_____
_____
_____
_____
_____
_____
_____
_____
_____
_____
_____
_____
_____

"Some objects are just things, but some carry the weight of love."
— Unknown

Items

Do you have a favorite childhood keepsake, and why is it special?

"What we treasure as children shapes who we become."
— Unknown

Grandchild, From My Heart to Yours

Items

Any objects you've created or collected that you hope will become heirlooms?

_____
_____
_____
_____
_____
_____
_____
_____
_____
_____
_____
_____
_____
_____
_____
_____

"Objects crafted with love become heirlooms in time."
— Unknown

Grandchild, From My Heart to Yours

Items

Do you have any treasured holiday decorations with a family story?

"Every decoration has a story, if you listen closely."
— *Unknown*

Grandchild, From My Heart to Yours

Items

What heirlooms do you hope future generations will cherish?

"What we pass down carries more than history—it carries love."
— Unknown

Items

What is your most cherished possession that you want to pass on and why?

"A family's story can be told through the things they cherish."
— *Unknown*

Grandchild, From My Heart to Yours

Items

What object that reminds you most of your childhood?

_____

_____

_____

_____

_____

_____

_____

_____

_____

_____

_____

_____

_____

_____

_____

"Our most valued possessions are often tied to our fondest memories."
— *Unknown*

Grandchild, From My Heart to Yours

Items

What are some special objects in our family that have been passed down?

"What we pass down defines who we are."
— Unknown

Grandchild, From My Heart to Yours

Items

Is there an item that best represents our family's values or beliefs? Describe it.

"A family's values are its greatest treasures."
— *Unknown*

Grandchild, From My Heart to Yours

Items

Are there objects that symbolize resilience or overcoming challenges?

"The strongest families carry the weight of history with pride."
— Unknown

Grandchild, From My Heart to Yours

Items

Describe any military medals or civic honors in the family.

Are there letters or documents from our ancestors that were preserved?

"A single lesson can change the course of a lifetime."
— Unknown

Grandchild, From My Heart to Yours

Items

Do you have any favorite photographs of us? Can you add a few below?

"Family photos remind us that time is fleeting, but love is eternal."
— Unknown

Share Your V.O.I.C.E.™

Counsel

Grandchild, From My Heart to Yours

Counsel

What's the best advice you ever received, and who gave it to you?

"Do what you love, and you'll never work a day in your life."
— *Confucius*

Grandchild, From My Heart to Yours
Counsel

How do you decide what truly matters?

"True happiness is found in the little things we often overlook."
— *Unknown*

Grandchild, From My Heart to Yours

Counsel

What advice would you give about staying true to your values?

"Your values define you more than your achievements."
— *Unknown*

Grandchild, From My Heart to Yours

Counsel

What do you think is the most important skill for success in life? And Why?

_____
_____
_____
_____
_____
_____
_____
_____
_____
_____
_____
_____
_____
_____

"Hard work beats luck every time."
— Unknown

Grandchild, From My Heart to Yours

Counsel

What's one thing you wish you had learned earlier in life?

"Mistakes are stepping stones, not roadblocks."
— Unknown

Grandchild, From My Heart to Yours

Counsel

What's your advice for living a meaningful life?

"A life well lived is one that leaves the world better than before."
— *Unknown*

Grandchild, From My Heart to Yours

Counsel

What's the most important lesson you've learned about love?

"Love grows when nurtured; neglect weakens it."
— Unknown

Grandchild, From My Heart to Yours

Counsel

What's essential to produce a happy marriage or partnership?

_____

_____

_____

_____

_____

_____

_____

What's the key to building strong family relationships?

_____

_____

_____

_____

_____

_____

_____

"Family bonds grow stronger when nurtured with time and care."
— Unknown

Grandchild, From My Heart to Yours

Counsel

What's one piece of advice you'd give about raising children?

What advice would you give about balancing work and family?

"Work is temporary; family is forever—prioritize accordingly."
— *Unknown*

Grandchild, From My Heart to Yours

Counsel

What advice do you have about achieving goals?

How do you know when to take risks?

"A goal without a plan is just a wish."
— *Antoine de Saint-Exupéry*

Grandchild, From My Heart to Yours

Counsel

How do you approach difficult decisions?

What's the best way to handle conflict in relationships?

"You'll never have all the answers—trust yourself to adapt."
— Unknown

Grandchild, From My Heart to Yours

Counsel

How do you manage stress in your daily life?

_____

_____

_____

_____

_____

_____

_____

How do you let go of things beyond your control?

_____

_____

_____

_____

_____

_____

_____

"Self-care isn't selfish; it's essential."
— Unknown

Grandchild, From My Heart to Yours

Counsel

What's your advice on how to handle regrets?

_____
_____
_____
_____
_____
_____
_____

What's the best way to recover from failure?

_____
_____
_____
_____
_____
_____
_____

"Failure is not the opposite of success; it's part of the journey."
— Unknown

Grandchild, From My Heart to Yours

Counsel

How do you stay true to yourself when facing criticism or adversity?

"Know your worth and don't let anyone tell you otherwise."
— Unknown

Grandchild, From My Heart to Yours

Counsel

What advice would you give to someone facing loss or grief?

"Grief is the price we pay for love."
— *Queen Elizabeth II*

Grandchild, From My Heart to Yours
Counsel

What's your best advice for being a good friend?

_____

_____

_____

_____

_____

_____

_____

_____

_____

_____

_____

_____

_____

_____

"A good friend listens with their heart, not just their ears."
— Unknown

Grandchild, From My Heart to Yours

Counsel

What advice would you give about handling life's challenges?

"Challenges are opportunities in disguise."
— *Unknown*

Grandchild, From My Heart to Yours

Counsel

What's the key to staying hopeful during tough times?

"Even the longest night will end, and the sun will rise."
— *Victor Hugo*

Grandchild, From My Heart to Yours

Counsel

Anything else you think your grandchild should know?

_____

_____

_____

_____

_____

_____

_____

_____

_____

_____

_____

_____

_____

_____

_____

"The world is a better place because you're in it."
— Unknown

Share Your V.O.I.C.E.™

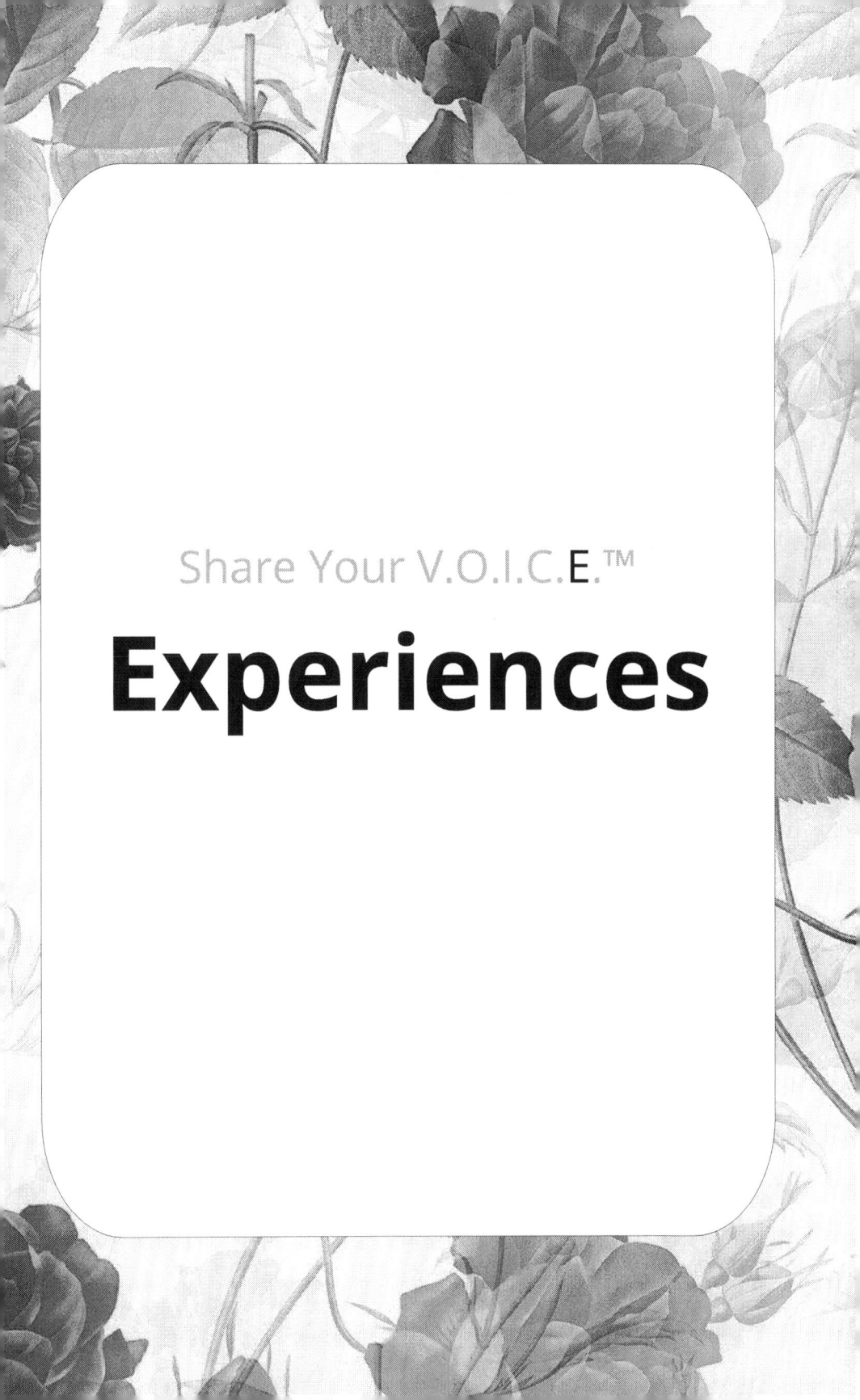

Experiences

Grandchild, From My Heart to Yours

Experiences

What is your earliest memory?

"Our earliest memories shape the foundation of who we are."
— Unknown

Grandchild, From My Heart to Yours

Experiences

Can you describe your childhood home?

"A childhood home is not just a place; it's a feeling."
— Unknown

Grandchild, From My Heart to Yours

Experiences

Can you share a story about your first job?

"The lessons from your first job often last a lifetime."
— *Unknown*

Grandchild, From My Heart to Yours

Experiences

Describe a favorite day you shared with your spouse or significant other.

"The best thing to hold onto in life is each other."
— Audrey Hepburn

Experiences

Can you describe becoming a parent for the first time?

"The moment you become a parent, your heart grows a thousand times bigger."
— Unknown

Grandchild, From My Heart to Yours

Experiences

Can you describe a family tradition you cherish?

"The simplest traditions often create the most meaningful memories."
— *Unknown*

Grandchild, From My Heart to Yours

Experiences

What's a story about a life lesson you learned the hard way?

"Life's toughest lessons leave the most lasting impressions."
— Unknown

Grandchild, From My Heart to Yours

Experiences

Can you describe a moment when you chose to be brave?

_____

_____

_____

_____

_____

_____

_____

_____

_____

_____

_____

_____

_____

_____

_____

_____

"Bravery is standing tall, even when your knees are shaking."
— Unknown

Grandchild, From My Heart to Yours

Experiences

What's a challenging moment you overcame?

"The struggles you face today will be the strength you rely on tomorrow."
— Unknown

Grandchild, From My Heart to Yours

Experiences

Can you describe a moment when you felt truly loved?

___

"Love wraps you in warmth, even in the coldest moments."
— Unknown

*Grandchild, From My Heart to Yours*

Experiences

Can you describe a moment when you felt like you truly succeeded?

"The greatest victories are the ones you achieve within yourself."
— *Unknown*

Grandchild, From My Heart to Yours

Experiences

Can you describe a time when your family came together to help each other?

_____

_____

_____

_____

_____

_____

_____

_____

_____

_____

_____

_____

_____

_____

_____

"In times of need, a family's love becomes its greatest strength."
— Unknown

Grandchild, From My Heart to Yours

Experiences

What's the funniest thing that ever happened to you?

"Humor is the spark that lights up the darkest days."
— Unknown

Grandchild, From My Heart to Yours

Experiences

What's a moment in your life that you wish you could relive?

_____
_____
_____
_____
_____
_____
_____
_____
_____
_____
_____
_____
_____
_____
_____
_____

"Some moments are so beautiful, they are worth reliving a thousand times."
— *Unknown*

Experiences

What's a moment that changed the course of your life?

"Life-changing moments teach us what we are truly capable of."
— Unknown

Grandchild, From My Heart to Yours

Experiences

What's a moment in life when you felt especially proud?

"Celebrate every milestone—it's a step forward in your journey."
— Unknown

Grandchild, From My Heart to Yours

Experiences

What's the most adventurous thing you've ever done?

"Dare to explore—it's the only way to truly live."
— *Unknown*

Grandchild, From My Heart to Yours

Experiences

Can you describe a moment that made you laugh uncontrollably?

_____

_____

_____

_____

_____

_____

_____

_____

_____

_____

_____

_____

_____

_____

_____

_____

"Laughter is the sound of the soul dancing."
— Jarod Kintz

Grandchild, From My Heart to Yours

Experiences

What would you consider your greatest achievement?

"Achievements are milestones on the journey of growth."
— Unknown

Grandchild, From My Heart to Yours

Experiences

Can you share a memory of a mentor who deeply influenced you?

_____

_____

_____

_____

_____

_____

_____

_____

_____

_____

_____

_____

_____

_____

_____

_____

"A mentor believes in you even when you don't believe in yourself."
— Unknown

Grandchild, From My Heart to Yours

Experiences

What's a story about a moment that gave your life new meaning?

"The most meaningful moments are the ones that transform your perspective."
— Unknown

Grandchild, From My Heart to Yours

Experiences

What's a memory about a time you felt completely at peace?

_____

_____

_____

_____

_____

_____

_____

_____

_____

_____

_____

_____

_____

_____

_____

"True peace is when your heart feels at home."
— Unknown

Grandchild, From My Heart to Yours

Experiences

What was the happiest moment of your life?

_____

_____

_____

_____

_____

_____

_____

_____

_____

_____

_____

_____

_____

"Happiness is when you realize you're exactly where you're meant to be."
— Unknown

Bonus Pages

More Thoughts

Grandchild, From My Heart to Yours

More Thoughts

Grandchild, From My Heart to Yours

More Thoughts

Grandchild, From My Heart to Yours

More Thoughts

Grandchild, From My Heart to Yours

More Thoughts

Grandchild, From My Heart to Yours

More Thoughts

About GrandparentsAcademy.com

Aaron Larsen founded GrandparentsAcademy.com (a.k.a. "Grandparents Academy") in 2011 while living with his Granny Grit. His grandparents' life-changing lessons and experiences inspired him to create the platform. After graduating college during the Great Recession, Aaron attended what he calls "Grand School," spending four years living with his grandparents in his early 20s. Determined to share and multiply the blessings he received from them, he launched the world's first online academy for grandparents, helping them build meaningful relationships and lasting legacies with their loved ones. As the global leader in grandparent education, Grandparents Academy has reached millions of grandparents worldwide.

These resources include masterclasses, memberships, and special events such as Grandparents Week, which is the largest online celebration and educational conference for grandparents of its kind.

There is truly something for every grandparent including: long distance grandparents, near and same town grandparents, estranged or alienated grandparents, grandparents raising their grandchildren, and others. Come take a look!

Get more resources at:
www.grandparentsacademy.com

Scan the QR code above with your phone or tablet for quick access.

Author Dedication:
I'm eternally grateful for my Grandma and Grandpa Grace + Granny and Grandpa Grit. Thank you for pouring into my life and always beleving in me, especially when I needed you most. Your legacy grows on.

~Aaron

ISBN: 979-8-9926099-0-5

©2025 Swiftrock LLC, GrandparentsAcademy.com, & Aaron Larsen. All rights reserved.

This book, *Grandchild, From My Heart to Yours: A Guided Journal & Family Keepsake*, and all content contained within, including but not limited to text, prompts, images, and design, are the intellectual property of Swiftrock LLC, GrandparentsAcademy.com, and Aaron Larsen and are protected under copyright law. No part of this publication may be reproduced, distributed, stored, or transmitted in any form or by any means—electronic, mechanical, photocopying, recording, or otherwise—without the prior written permission of the publisher, except in the case of brief quotations for the purpose of review or commentary.

This book is intended for personal use only. Any commercial use, including but not limited to resale, reproduction for distribution, or use in workshops, seminars, or other instructional settings without authorization, is strictly prohibited.

The information and prompts within this book are designed as a guided journaling experience and are provided for educational and personal reflection purposes. The publisher and author assume no responsibility for how the information is used.

For permissions, inquiries, or licensing requests, please contact: **support@grandparentsacademy.com**

Made in United States
Troutdale, OR
03/25/2025